# Me

by

Carol Muia

RoseDog Books
PITTSBURGH, PENNSYLVANIA 15238

RoseDog Books
585 Alpha Drive
Suite 103
Pittsburgh, PA 15238
Visit our website at *www.rosedogbookstore.com*

ISBN: 978-1-4809-7606-1
eISBN: 978-1-4809-7629-0

# Me

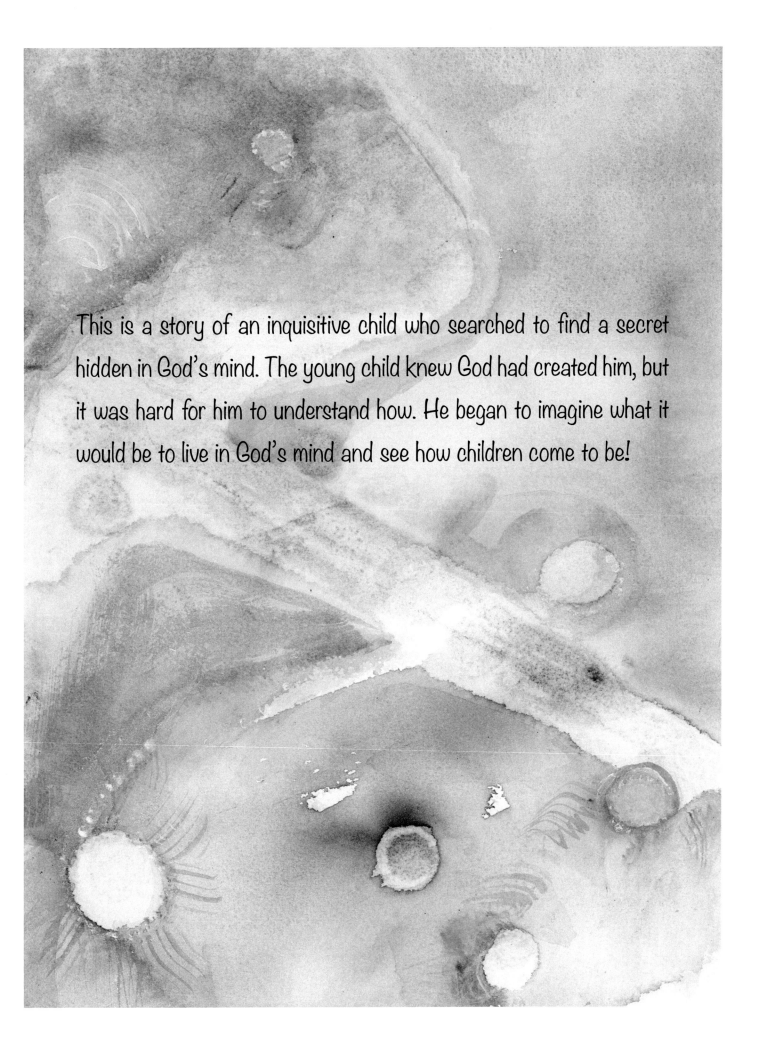

This is a story of an inquisitive child who searched to find a secret hidden in God's mind. The young child knew God had created him, but it was hard for him to understand how. He began to imagine what it would be to live in God's mind and see how children come to be!

Do you know who I am?

Silly looking me

I am a thought in God's mind

Of a child to be!

God will form me

Carefully make each part

And when He is finished...

He will breathe love into my heart!

God created all things. Some great, some small…

But He loved little children as His best thought of all.

When I think of all this it puzzles me
Was I really a thought in God's mind
Before God made me, ME?

I
WONDER...

What did I look like when I was a thought
in God's mind?
Did I look kind of strange a blob of some
kind?

Did I look like this without form or design?
And was it fun to be a thought in God's mind?

I began to imagine... Imagine all that I might see
If I could just pretend to be a thought of a child to be.

No longer a child but a thought in God's mind
And now I could see Great things of all kind!
Maybe see things only God's eyes see
Watch Him make children out of thoughts like you and me!

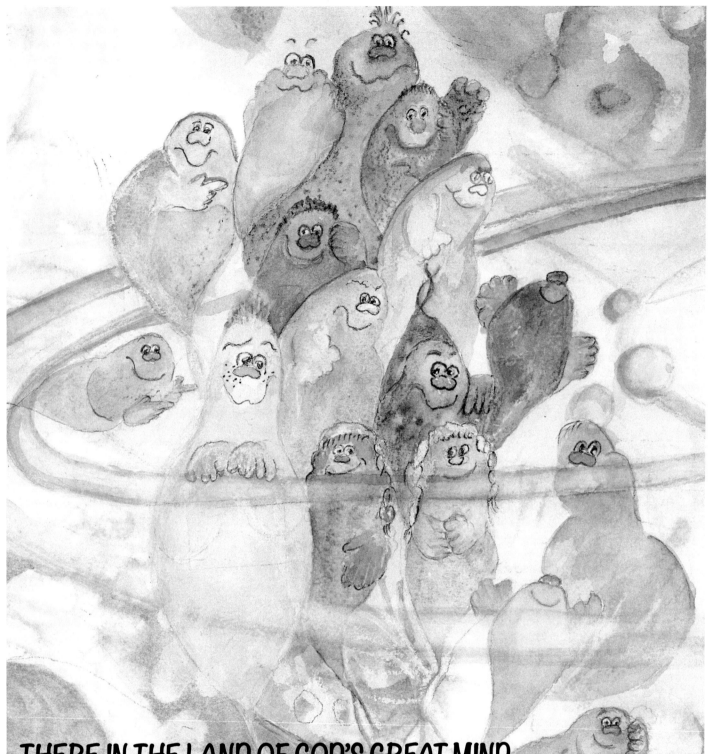

# THERE IN THE LAND OF GOD'S GREAT MIND.

I could see thoughts of every color and kind.

Not one was like another, each one different, unlike any other.

I was different, too, no one quite like me - a child to be with so much curiosity!

All day long I searched to find
How God makes a child
with just a thought in His mind.
But I did not find the answer.
No! I did not
And I needed to find the answer
Because it puzzled me a lot!
I wonder if the others know?
I will ask and see
If they know about children...
I'm sure they will tell me!

Slowly I flew over
To where the others were at play
And I said to them in a friendly way

"Excuse me, please, for interrupting," I said
"But a very strange question puzzles my head!
This question may seem silly, and it is in a way
But I need to know the answer so I'll ask anyway.

Have you seen or heard... do you know maybe...
How God makes children out of thoughts like you and me?"
They shrugged their shoulders "no," shook each head,
"We know nothing about children," they sighed and said.

"You know nothing about children!" was my loud reply.
"Then we must find answers and I will tell you why!
How can we become children when we don't know how to grow?
How can we go to earth when we don't know where to go?"

"I do know how, now!"
I laughed out loud and said
"Because something I forgot
just popped into my head!
I forgot we are pretend thoughts,
I totally forgot.
Forgot we can do things
other thoughts cannot!
We can do anything, go anywhere...
Imagination will take us everywhere!"

"See all those pathways,"
I pointed, "running through God's head?
We are going to see where they lead!" I said.
"Maybe we'll see things only God's eyes see...
Watch Him make children
out of thoughts like you and me!

So get ready for adventure
and lots of fun!"
And off I started
in a fast-forward run!
My new friends
followed way far behind...
They were not at all,
the adventurous kind!

"Hurry!" I shouted. "Come quickly and see
Sparkling pathways straight ahead of me!"
My friends hurried to be by my side,
And together we entered and went inside!

Our eyes could not believe
What we saw...
We moved quietly and slowly
And looked around in awe.
Off in the distance we heard a happy sound
And it grew louder and filled the air all around.

The happy sounds grew louder and filled the air
Sounds of happy play time were everywhere

Sounds of laughter...
Happy fun...
Like noisy games
Had just begun.

"Look!" I cried. "Look! Can you see what I see?
What is this awesome land... what can it be?"

"I don't know," I whispered. "I cannot see anyone

All I hear are voices of someone having fun!

I guess we should go closer and quietly look

around.

See who is making all that happy sound!"

Quietly together, hand in hand

Together we entered the mysterious land.

Our eyes looked up and down and all about...
And when we saw who made the noise...our eyes popped out!

I wanted to ask questions, but I could not talk.
I just stood there with a dumbfounded gawk!

The one standing closest looked at me and smiled.
Suddenly my words burst out, "Are you a child?
Are you a child? Could it be true?
Someday, one day, will I look like you?"

The one smiling at me smiled a still bigger smile
"Yes!" she answered. "I am a child.
We are all children here, but, please understand...
This is not Earth... this is the 'Children's Land!'
A land of happiness where all wishes come true
God invited me to live here the others too."

"Earth is there"...she pointed, "see far away...
I lived there...the others too! So will you someday."

I will tell you a story, so you will understand...
"How thoughts become children in that far away land."

"One day," her story began.
"I don't remember when...

When God decided
My life should begin...

God gathered His thoughts of children to be
And on that day, He chose me!"

"He picked me up and put me into a seed to grow
And He planted that seed on the earth below."

"I formed and grew and soon
was ready for birth
And on that day, God looked
down on earth..."

He breathed His breath
And oh, how He smiled...
There on earth
His very own child!"

"And there," said she.
"I lived for a while..."
And she gave me another
Very big smile.

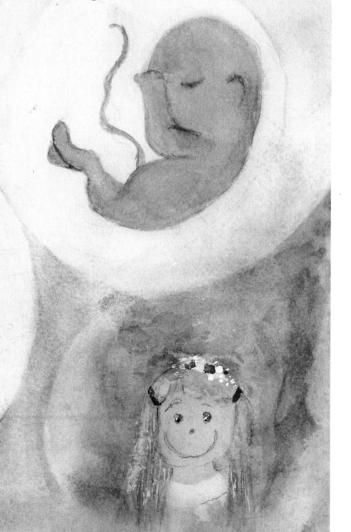

"Now," said she, with a very big grin,
"My story telling has come to an end."
She glanced over at the others,
who were standing close by
And everyone was grinning,
but no one said why!

Everyone grinning in a mysterious way...
As if they all knew a secret they could not give away

SOON, VERY SOON I FOUND OUT...
WHAT ALL THE GRINNING WAS ALL ABOUT!

The children disappeared
Not even my friends were there...
All my eyes could see...
was the bright starlit air!

"Come back!" I cried out. "Please, please do.
I want to know how to disappear, too!"

I did not know, I did not see
The great surprise
God had planned for me!
He picked me up and put me
Into a seed to grow...
And he planted the seed
On the earth below.

I grew and formed
And was soon ready for birth.
And on that day
God looked down on earth...
He breathed His breath and oh how He smiled
Here on Earth, ME! His very own child!

Awesome to imagine that before I was me

I was a thought in God's mind, a child to be!

Could this really be true? I wonder...maybe so, maybe not...

But if it is true, something puzzles me a lot!

What happened to my friends, the friends I left behind?

Do they live here on earth somewhere or are they still in God's mind?

I think I know the answer
because just today
My parents said to me,
in a very excited way...

"Our family is about to grow.
In fact it will grow by twos.
We're having twins,
yes twins," they said.
"We hope you like the news!"

Minds that can imagine have eyes to see...
some things that possibly just might be!